THE PRAYING WIFE

AN INTRODUCTION
TO EFFECTIVE PRAYER

MELTORIA A. WOODSIDE

Copyright © 2020 Meltoria Woodside

All rights reserved.

ISBN:

DEDICATION

To all the wives who are facing crisis in their marriages and families, I dedicated this book to you. The decision to fight for your marriage and family is easy. Staying in the fight and making the changes and adjustments necessary to position yourself and persevere through the fight, that is difficult!

However, you made the decision that you will take the journey for your marriage. Although you may not be able to see it now, let me encourage you. You are stronger than you know

ACKNOWLEDGEMENT

First off, I want to acknowledge Lord, the Holy Spirit, my helper and my guide. I certainly could not write this book without His divine help and guidance.

Then I want to acknowledge my beloved husband Yocasta Woodside Sr, who is always pushing, supporting, and encouraging me in everything that I set out to do.

Then I want to acknowledge me wonderful boys, they keep me pumped and excited. The face that they
make when I accomplish things that I set out to accomplish is priceless.

CONTENTS

DEDICATION..iii

ACKNOWLEDGEMENT iv

1. LORD TEACH ME TO PRAY 1
2. THE PRECEDENT FOR PRAYER................................4
3. HOW OFTEN SHOULD WE PRAY 9
4. TYPES OF PRAYERS... 11
5. PRAYER & THE HEART.................................... 16
6. ASK IN MY NAME.. 22
7. 10 BIBLICAL NAMES OF GOD 25
8. KEYS TO ANSWERED PRAYERS 29
9. THE HOUR OF PRAYER.. 35
10. (PRAYER WATCH).. 35
11. THE 8 PRAYER WATCHES 39
12. PRAYER ESSENTIALS 46
13. PRAYER GUIDENCE 50
14. PRAYER FOR YOUR MARRIAGE............................. 57

15. PRAYER FOR WISDOM 64

16. PRAYER FOR VINDICATION AND ANGELIC HELP 68

17. PRAYERS THAT ROUT DEMONS 72

ABOUT THE AUTHOR... 78

OTHER BOOKS BY THE AUTHOR. 81

LORD TEACH ME TO PRAY

One day as Jesus was praying in a certain place, when he finished one of his disciples said to him, "Lord teach us to pray just as John taught his disciples." (Luke 11:1).

Why did the disciples ask Jesus to teach them to pray?

Because they understood that there was a pattern, to be effective in prayer and they needed to learn that pattern.

We all can agree that when you are looking for someone to teach you something, that means that they know something that you want or need to learn.

When you learn how to pray effectively you will not get burned out, you will not have to drag yourself to pray, neither will you be on every prayer line seeking prayer.

In fact, you will be encouraged, excited, always motivated and always in anticipation for prayer.

The most effective person to pray for your marriage and family is you. Corporate prayer is great, corporate prayer is powerful, however when you have personal needs you must learn to pray.

Prayer is a weapon, and it is especially necessary when you are in a bottle of some sort.

For the weapons of our warfare are not carnal, but mighty through God to the pulling down of strong holds. (2 Corinthians 10:4)

There is a battle that is going on, believe it or not, you are in that battle. It is up to you if you are going to stand up and fight or sit back and be defeated.

To fight this battle, you must learn to praise and worship, declare God's word, have faith and pray.

Prayer is not something you do only when you need something from God, or having trouble, because prayer is all offensive and defensive.

Then Jesus told his disciples a parable to show them that they should always pray and not give up.

Luke 18:1.

Prayer will cause you to see an attack before it comes. Then you will be prepared for whatever comes your way. The enemy will attack, but because of active prayer his attack will not be as effective as it would be if there was no prayer.

THE PRECEDENT FOR PRAYER

When Jesus' disciple asked Him to teach them to pray, He responded with a prayer that would be the precedent, which we should follow for effective prayer.

We all know this prayer as the "The Lord's Prayer".

Although Jesus responded with this prayer, this is not the only prayer that we should pray.

However, this prayer shows us the pattern of how we should be praying.

Not only were the disciples given the format of prayer, but they were also given the protocol of what we need to do when we fix our hearts to pray.

We do not need to be seen, we do not need a platform or stage to pray. The most effective way to pray is to pray in the secret place.

'And when you pray, you must not be like the hypocrites. For they love to stand and pray in the synagogues and at the street corners, that they may be seen by others. Truly, I say to you, they have received their reward. 6 But when you pray, go into your room, and shut the door and pray to your Father who is in secret. And your Father who sees in secret will reward you.' (Matthew 6:5-6)

Jesus also taught, that having many words does not mean that you are praying properly.

Many words have no effect if what you are saying is nothing but a lot of phrases that sound good.

'And when you pray, do not heap up empty phrases as the Gentiles do, for they think that they will be heard for their many words. Do not be like them, for your Father knows what you need before you ask him. Pray then like this: (Matthew 6:8)

The Lord's Prayer

Our Father, which art in heaven, Hallowed be thy

Name. Thy Kingdom comes. Thy will be done in earth, as it is in heaven. Give us this day our daily bread. And forgive us our trespasses, as we forgive them that trespass against us. And lead us not into temptation but deliver us from evil. For thine is the kingdom, The power, and the glory, For ever and ever. Amen.

(Matthew 6:9:15)

Let us understand what Jesus was teaching through this prayer.

Our Father, which art in heaven, hallowed be thy name – Praise & Worship

When we enter prayer, we must follow the protocol of worship.

Enter into His gates with thanksgiving, And into His courts with praise. Be thankful to Him and bless His name.

(Psalm 100:4)

Thy Kingdom comes, thy will be done on earth as it is in heaven. – The Will of God

The Lord seeks to perform His word, His word is His will. When we pray, we must pray the will of God.

The LORD said to me, "You have seen correctly, for

I am watching to see that my word is fulfilled." (Jeremiah 1:12)

Give us this day our daily bread – Petition.

The Lord knows what we need even before we ask.

However, we are still instructed to ask Him to provide what we need and to sustain us from day to day.

"Ask, and it shall be given you; seek, and ye shall find; knock, and it shall be opened unto you:" (Matthew 7:7)

And forgive us our trespasses, as we forgive them that trespass against us – Repent of sins and forgive others of their sin against you.

Repentance is important in prayer, because we do not want our sins standing between us and God.

And according to the scripture, if we want to be forgiven, we must also forgive.

"For if you forgive other people when they sin against you, your heavenly Father will also forgive you." (Matthew 6:14)

And lead us not into temptation but deliver us from evil – Petition and Deliverance

For thine is the kingdom, the power, and the glory, forever and ever. Amen – Praise & Worship

HOW OFTEN SHOULD WE PRAY

Pray without ceasing.

> *"Rejoice at all times. Pray without ceasing. Give thanks in every circumstance, for this is God's will for you in Christ Jesus...." (1Thessalonians 5:16-*
>
> *18)*
>
> *KJV - "Praying always with all prayer and supplication in the Spirit, and watching thus with all perseverance and supplication for all saints;*
>
> *(Ephesians 6:18)*
>
> *NIV - "And pray in the Spirit on all occasions with all kinds of prayers and requests. With*

this in mind, be alert and always keep on praying for all the

Lord's people." (Ephesians 6:18)

The book of Ephesians teaches us a whole lot about instructions that we need to have been given about prayer.

- Pray always - Just as mentioned in Luke 18:1 - Pray all prayers or all kinds of prayers.

Throughout the scriptures we would find different types of prayers prayed. If you are going to be effective in prayer, you must know what kind of prayer you need to pray based on what you want to accomplish.

When we consider the context of what Paul wrote, we recognize that Paul was not instructing believers to give up their responsibilities and only pray.

Rather, this passage teaches us that we need to commit ourselves to prayer and make it a top priority in our lives.

By making prayer a top priority, we will remain holy and pure, having hearts ready for when Jesus returns.

Prayer helps us stay accountable to living righteously.

TYPES OF PRAYERS

Warfare Prayer - In this type of prayer you are engaging the enemy. As a Christian you must know your authority.

However, when you get into spiritual warfare, you must know your place. The realm of the spirit and the natural are governed by laws, and we must always be careful that we are operated within the parameters of these laws.

If we do not, we will experience backlash or unnecessary warfare.

But even the archangel Michael, when he was disputing with the devil about the body of Moses, did not himself dare to condemn him for slander, but said,

"the Lord rebuke you." (Jude 1:9)

Prayer Nugget - You cannot rebuke Satan, but you can ask the Lord to rebuke him.

Words of Wisdom - If you are struggling in an area personally, deal with that area before you go advising other people affected in that area too.

Why? If you do not, it will lead to an increased confusion on your part.

For how will you go to remove a speck in another person's eyes, while ignoring the log of wood in your own eyes?

It's not done that way.

For example, if you are having problems in your marriage, do not engage in spiritual warfare for others, or try to bring peace back to other marriages. You will increase warfare for yourself and your marriage.

In Acts 19:11-16, It talks about the sons of Scevea, who tried to operate on a level they were not ranked for.

They saw the Apostle Paul being used by God then suddenly, they thought they were equipped to do the same thing.

However, they came under attack by the very demons they were trying to fight or cast out.

Seven sons of Sceva, a Jewish chief priest, were doing this. One day the evil spirit answered them, "Jesus I know, and Paul I know about, but who are you? Then the man who had the evil spirit jumped on them and overpowered them all. He gave them such a beating that they ran out of the house naked and bleeding. (Acts 19:14-16)

Prayer of Deliverance - Prayer of deliverance is necessary when you need to be free of a thing that is holding you bound.

Prayer of deliverance is necessary when you are being demonically oppressed by an evil spirit.

Whenever we are bound by a spirit or spirits, that means that they would have had a legal right to afflict you.

To be free, you must remove the legal right and then cast them out.

How is this done?

This is Done by identifying the root cause of the issue or identifying where the legal right was given.

Then you must renounce it or repent from that issue then ask for help. Once you want help, the Holy Spirit will help you.

Supplication Prayer - This are the personal prayers we say to God for our own life. Personal supplication prayer is the type that we tell our problems to God with a solemn heart.

The prayer of Jabez is a great example of supplication prayer. Jabez cried out to the God of

Israel, and said,

"Oh, that you would bless me and enlarge my territory! Let your hand be with me and keep me from harm so that I will be free from pain." And God granted his request. (Chronicles 4:10)

Prayer of Faith – The prayer of faith is when you are in a place, a certainty without a shadow of doubt that what you are requesting for would be granted.

Luke 17:6 tells us that if you have faith as small as a mustard seed, you can say to this mulberry tree, be pulled up by the roots and be planted in the sea, it will obey you.

This prayer is a powerful prayer, because when you pray in faith not only will you have what you ask for, but it is pleasing to God.

And without faith it is impossible to please God because anyone who comes to him must believe that he exists and that he rewards those who earnestly seek him. (Hebrews 11:6).

The prayer of faith lies within our confidence and trust in the Lord and His word. If you are in a place where you lack faith to pray this type of prayer, do not be discouraged. Faith is freely available to you.

Romans 10:17 tells us that faith comes by hearing and hearing by the word of God.

Hearing is translated from the Greek word akoe which means the act, the sense or the thing heard). Hearing is a continuous action. If you are going to get faith from God's word, there must be a continuous action of hearing it. Read it, ponder on it and memorize it.

PRAYER & THE HEART

The heart is the feelings, the will, the intellect center. The heart is the flesh.

What is in your heart (your feelings, your will and your intellect) is not what is in God's feelings, His Will or His intellect.

"For my thoughts are not your thoughts, neither are your ways my ways, declares the Lord. For as the heavens are higher than the earth, so my ways are higher than your ways and my thoughts than your thoughts."
(Isaiah 55:8-9)

"But those things which proceed out of the mouth come from the heart, and they defile the man."

(Matthew 15:18)

- Many are being defiled by their prayers.

- Yes, your prayers are what you speak, and according to Matthew 15:18, what you speak defile you.

- What you speak out of your mouth is what is in our heart. If your heart is unhealthy so will your words be. For out of the abundance of the heart the mouth speaks.

A good man brings good things out of the good stored up in his heart, and an evil man brings evil things out of the evil stored up in his heart.

For the mouth speaks what the heart is full of.

Luke 6:45

- In fact, therefore it is important to be led by the spirit when you are praying from the place of hurt, brokenness or pain.

Your heart will have you praying from the realm of the flesh and your prayers will never get answered.

When our prayers are unanswered, we get frustrated and discouraged. Then eventually we stop praying.

NIV - The heart is deceitful above all things and beyond cure who can understand it? Jeremiah 17:9

NLT - The human heart is the most deceitful of all things, and desperately wicked. Who really knows how bad it is? Jeremiah 17:9

Your heart is so deceitful, that you can passionately pray using scripture to back your prayer, and you can still be out of the will of God.

God will not answer any prayers that are outside of his will or against His word.

Here is an example.

Early on in ministry, I have encountered a whole lot of women praying for, and against the woman who was the center of their marital issues.

Many of those women expressed how draining they were from praying. Many expressed how discouraged they were because prayers seem to not be working.

To my natural man, I honestly believed that these prayers were selfless prayers. However, by the time I consulted the Holy Spirit, I realized that these kind selfless prayers were against the will of God in these matters.

Here is why.

When spiritual laws are broken, the hand of God moves on, these matters and most of the time the judgement is already rendered, and no prayer can change it.

Also, scripture tells us that it is not the will of God that none should perish.

The LORD is not slow in keeping his promise, as some understand slowness.

Instead he is patient with you, not wanting anyone to perish, but everyone to come to repentance. (2 Peter 3:9)

In the story of Balak & Balaam. Balaam said, "How can I curse those whom God has not cursed? How can I condemn those whom the Lord has not condemned?" (Numbers 23:8)

During the time I was in the fight for my marriage, one prayer I did not pray was the prayer for or against the other women.

However, God moved greatly on my behalf, nonetheless.

In Psalm 51:10 David said "Create in me a pure heart, O God, and renew a right spirit within me."

David understood he had issues within his heart and needed God to renew it.

Many of us have or had heart issues. Although your heart issue may not have been your fault, it is important that you deal with your heart issue because if you do not, they will hinder your prayers.

Your prayers must be balanced, because the Holy Spirit will help you. Eventually you will be led in the right direction to deal with those issues.

"Search me O God and know my heart; test me and know my concerns. See if there is any offensive way in me; lead me in the way everlasting." (Psalm 139:23-24)

Just as we must pray always, we must always put our heart before the Lord for examination. He is the one that can see if there is any offensive way in it.

But the Lord said to Samuel, "do not consider his appearance or his height, for I have rejected him."

The Lord does not look at things people look at. People look at the outward appearance, but the Lord looks at the heart. 1 Samuel 16:7

ASK IN MY NAME

Name: the name is used for everything which the NAME covers, everything the thought or feeling of which is aroused in the mind by mentioning, hearing, and remembering.

Example the name for one's rank, authority, interest, pleasure, command, excellences, deed. Etc.

Knowing who Jesus is will cause you to be effective in prayer. Because he said if you ask in my name "That will I do".

"And whatsoever ye shall ask in my name, that will I do, that the Father may be glorified in the Son." John

14:13

When Jesus said, "Ask in my name". He did not limit us to Jesus the Christ or Yeshua Hamashiach.

How do I know? Because Isaiah said He would be called wonderful, Counselor, The Mighty God, Everlasting Father and Prince of Peace.

"For unto us a child is born, unto us a son is given: and the government shall be upon his shoulder: and his name shall be called Wonderful, Counselor, The mighty God, The everlasting Father, The Prince of

Peace." Isaiah 9:6

In Isaiah 9:6, Name is translated as Shem (Shame). Through the idea of definite and conspicuous position.

An appellation, as a mark or memorial of individuality, by implication honor, authority, character.

When God was sending Moses to set his people free, Moses asked, "Who shall I say is sending me?"

"And Moses said unto God behold when I come unto the children of Israel, and shall say unto them the God of your fathers had sent me unto you and they shall say to me, what is his name? What shall I say unto them? And God said unto Moses, 'I am that I am'." Exodus 3:13-14

Now, all this is just a foundation to show you how vast

Jesus' name is and give you an understanding of His identity as it relates to what He is called and how we can tie His name into our prayer.

Very truly I tell you, Jesus answered before

Abraham was born. John 8:58

"In the beginning was the word and the word was with God and the word was God, He was with God in the beginning through Him all things were made and without Him nothing was made that has been made." John 1:1-

10 BIBLICAL NAMES OF GOD

1. El Shaddi - God Almighty – God's name, El Shaddai, reminds us that He is all-powerful, He is the Mighty One.

"Whoever dwells in the shelter of the Most

High will rest in the shadow of the Almighty." Psalm

91:1

"And when Abram was ninety years old and nine, the Lord appeared to Abram and said unto him, I am the ALMIGHTY GOD." Genesis 17:1

2. Elohim - This name refers to God's incredible power and might. He is the One and only

God. He is Supreme, the true God

"In the Beginning God created heaven and the earth." Genesis 1:1

3. Jehovah Jireh (Yireh) - The Lord will provide

The name Jehovah Jireh reminds us that in a time of need God provides for us. Whatever the need is, we need to remember that there is nothing too hard for the Lord.

"And Abraham called the name of that place

Jehovah Jireh: as it said this day on the   mount of the

Lord it shall be seen." Genesis 22:14

4. Rapha (Jehovah Rapha) - The Lord that heals

He said, "If you listen carefully to the

LORD your God and do what is right in his eyes, if you pay attention to his commands and keep all his decrees, I will not bring on you any of the diseases I brought on the Egyptians, for I am the LORD, who heals you." Exodus 15:26

5. Phos (light) John 8:12

"Then spoke Jesus again unto them saying,

I am the Light of the world, he that follow me shall not walk in darkness but shall have the light of life."

6. Yahweh "The Lord" Exodus 3:13-14

Yahweh is derived from the Hebrew word " I AM". It is the proper name of the divine person, coming from the verb which means to "exist".

And God said unto Moses, "I AM THAT I AM", and He said, "you will say this to the children of Israel, 'I AM has sent me to you".

7. ABBA - Daddy, Father Galatians 4:6 ABBA is the most intimate form of God's name, showing us His character as a Loving father.

"Because you are his sons, God sent the Spirit of His son into our hearts, the Spirit who calls out,

ABBA, Father."

8. El Elyon "God Most High" Psalm 7:17

El Elyon is used to reveal God as the God above all gods, that nothing in life is more sacred.

"I will praise the Lord according to His righteousness: and will sing praises to the name of the

Lord most High."

9. Jehovah Shammah – The Lord who is there, The Lord is present (Ezekiel 48:35)

10. Jehovah Gibbor Milchamah

"Who is this King of glory? The LORD strong and mighty, the LORD mighty in battle."

Psalm 24:8

KEYS TO ANSWERED PRAYERS

Within this scripture lies five keys that will help you get your prayers answered in matters relating to your marriage.

Now this is not for everyone, this is for the people of God. As the scripture says, those which are called by my name.

"If my people, who are called by my name, will humble themselves and pray and seek my face and turn from their wicked ways, then I will hear from heaven, and I will forgive their sin and will heal their land." (2 Chronicles 7:14)

Who is God's people?

Those who belong to the household of faith.

- "As we have therefore the opportunity, let us do good unto all men, especially unto them who are of the household of faith." Galatians 6:10 KJV

Therefore, as we have the opportunity, let us do good to all people, especially to those who belong to the family of believers. NIV

1. The first key is humility – You have got to humble yourself.

To humble means to be brought low, be under, be brought into subjection, be subdued.

Humility is a process, a process that can happen by fasting. This is not an overnight process, so do not think that one fast will humble you.

In order to humble yourself you must get rid of pride.

C.S. Lewis describes humility not as thinking less of ourselves, but as thinking of ourselves less.

But he gives more grace. Therefore, it says, "God opposes the proud but gives grace to the humble."

James 4:6

When you humble yourself, you challenge your motives?

You ask yourself, "Am I doing this for God or am I doing this for me?

Am I faithfully praying for my marriage because I don't want to go through this misery or hell? Or Do I want God to use this as an opportunity to demonstrate His glory?"

2. The 2nd key is Prayer – You must learn to pray. Prayer is how we address God.

In this passage, to pray means to intervene, interpose, to intercede.

• When you are interceding, you are not praying about your needs, but you are standing on behalf of others.

Luke 18:1-1, Jesus told his disciples a parable to show them that they should always pray and not give up.

3. The 3rd Key is Seek God's Face. – When you seek God's face you are looking to know Him. And that is building a relationship with Him, to know who He is, what He is about, what He wants, what He like, what He do not like, what He want!

When you seek God, He will reward you.

"But without faith it is impossible to please Him, for he who comes to God must believe that He is, and that He is a rewarder of those who diligently seek

Him." Hebrews 11:6

Diligent – to seek out for one's self, crave, search for, to seek out e.g. investigate, scrutinize.

If you draw near to God, He will also draw near to you.

"Draw nigh to God, and he will draw nigh to you. Cleanse your hands, ye sinners; and purify your hearts, ye double minded." James 4:8

4. The 4th key is to turn from your wicked ways. – turning from your wicked ways is to pursue righteousness!

This righteousness is not our righteousness but the righteousness of God.

"But we are all as an unclean thing, and all our righteousness's are as filthy rags; and we all do fade as a leaf; and our iniquities, like the wind, have taken us away." Isaiah 64:6

Matthew 6:33 33 says, "But seek first his kingdom and his righteousness, and all these things will be given to you as well."

When I came to that place where I said,

"God, I surrender to you!"

And I decided that I was going to seek God's face and stop seeking His hands. The First thing God did was lead me to get HEALING & DELIVERANCE.

God wanted to bless me and answer my prayers, but my filth was before him!

5. The 5th key is Patience – When we have done what is expected of us, then we must wait on the Lord.

"Wait for the LORD; be strong and take heart and wait for the LORD." Psalm 27:14

If you have an issue with patience, then you need to submit yourself to the Holy Spirit, so that He can deal with your impatience.

"But the fruit of the Spirit is love, joy, peace, forbearance, kindness, goodness, faithfulness, gentleness and self-control. Against such things there is no law." Galatians 5:22-23

Pray ask God to give you patience!

You may have been a good friend of impatience all your life, well let me tell you, it is about that time for you to let that relationship go.

Because it will not cause God to move on your behalf any soon than He plan.

"He hath made everything beautiful in his time: also, he hath set the world in their heart, so that no man can find out the work that God maketh from the beginning to the end." Ecclesiastes 3:11

Galatians 6:9 9 says, "Let us not become weary in doing good, for at the proper time we will reap a harvest if we do not give up."

THE HOUR OF PRAYER

(PRAYER WATCH)

What is a prayer watch?

A prayer watch is a specific time in the spiritual realm when specific demands, commands and request are obeyed or granted

"Watch and pray, that ye enter not into temptation; the spirit indeed is willing, but the flesh is weak."

(Matthew 26:41)

Watch is translated as (Grēgoreō) – This means to keep awake, be vigilant, be watchful, give strict attention to, be cautious, be active.

Matthew 26:41 says, "He's giving us a tool and strategy to keep us from falling into temptation and that is to watch, to be vigilant, be cautious, keep awake and pray."

"But while men slept, his enemy came and sowed tares among the wheat and went his way." (Matthew

13:25)

When I began to understand the prayer watch, my eyes were opened. I was then able to see just how the enemy was able to come in my house and cause destruction.

I WAS ASLEEP!

I was spiritually asleep and unaware of what the enemy was doing in my marriage and in my life.

When we pray always, we can not only grow spiritually or stay in communication with God, but prayer builds a hedge of protection.

When there is a hedge of protection the enemy cannot touch you!

Satan answered the Lord, "Does Job fear God for nothing? Have you not placed a hedge on every side around him and his household and all that he owns? You have blessed the work of his hands, and his possessions have increased in the land." (Job 1:9-11)

Job was a man that made sacrifices to the Lord "Just in case" on behalf of his family. He was proactive and not reactive and because of this the Lord considered him "Blameless & Upright"

The attack on Jobs life was not because he was falling short, the attack upon his life was because he was blameless and upright before the Lord.

"But know this, that if the master of the house hand known what hour the thief would come, he would have watched and not all his house to be broken into."

(Matthew 24:43)

In this passage, Jesus is giving words of pity to the owner of the house. Basically saying, "If he had kept watch he would have known when the enemy was coming".

If the owner was prayerful, he would have been alert and vigilant and be able to see when an attack was coming to his house.

If you are going to be awake or if you want to be awake. You must devote at least 1 hour to prayer every day.

Then Jesus returned to the disciples and found them

sleeping. "Are you not able to keep watch with me for one hour, He asked peter?" (Matthew 26:40)

Knowing these prayer watches will help us to pray the right prayers at the right time!

THE 8 PRAYER WATCHES

There are eight prayer watches with our physical 24-hour period. Each watch is a summation of 3 hours. The spiritual realm does not count hours as we do.

The 1st Watch – 6pm – 9pm

During this watch it is a time for reflection. Reflection on the goodness of God. Thinking about all He has done the day before. You should give prayers of thanksgiving during this time.

Also, at this time you should also reflect on the things that you should not have done.

Therefore, prayers of repentance should be done during this time.

Prayer of repentance is vital during the start of the prayer watch because it removes anything that may hinder the prayers that may follow this time.

But your iniquities have separated you from your God; your sins have hidden his face from you, so that he will not hear. (Isaiah 59:2)

The 2nd Watch 9pm – 12am (Night Watch) During this time is a time for prayers of adoration.

Lifting and glorying the name of the Lord giving high praises to Him. Knowing the names of God is necessary, and highly effective during this hour.

"And having prayed toward midnight Paul and Silas praised God in a hymn and the prisoners listened to them. And suddenly there was a great earthquake, so that the foundations of the jail were shaken. And immediately all the doors were opened, and all of the bonds were loosened." (Acts 16:25 – 26)

The 3rd Watch – 12am – 3am

The third watch is one of the difficult watches. It is the watch where there is much warfare.

Occult and demonic activity is high during this watch because it is the time when men are usually deep in sleep.

Therefore, the enemy uses this time to sow seeds of destruction in our lives.

"But while everyone was sleeping, his enemy came and sowed weeds among the wheat and went away."

(Matthew 13:25)

Warfare Prayers are the prayers for this hour. If you are called to this hour of prayer, be sure you are prepared for war.

During this time is the time to pray for Government, Marriage & Family.

"It will be good for those servants whose master finds them watching when he comes. Truly I tell you, he will dress himself to serve, will have them recline at the table and will come and wait on them. 38It will be good for those servants whose master finds them ready, even if he comes in the middle of the night or toward daybreak." (Luke 12:37 – 38)

The 4th Watch (3am – 6am)

During this hour is when the darkness recedes. The wicked forces flee and go back into their secret places.

Light takes dominion and forces the darkness away.

"And the light shines in the darkness and darkness did not comprehend it."(John 1:5)

"You are the light you have the ability to force the darkness back.

You are the light of the world. A city on a hill cannot be hidden." (Matthew 5:14)

During the fourth watch is also a good time to inquire of the Lord. Are you confused about something? Do you need revelation? Then arise at the fourth watch and pray!

"O God you are my God; early will I seek you; my soul thirst for you, my flesh faints for you in a dry and thirsty land with no water." (Psalm 63:1)

The 5th Watch (6am – 9am Morning Watch)

During this watch is a time to be still and listen to what the Lord is speaking.

"Be still and know that I am God; I will be exalted among the nations; I will be exalted in the earth."

(Psalm 46:10) If you will be intentional about listening

for the voice of the Lord. Most certainly if you have never heard him speak before, surely you will hear him during this time.

"I will stand at my watch and station myself on the watchtower and I will keep watch to see what He will say to me and with I will answer when I am reproved." (Habakuk 2:1)

The 6th Watch (9am -12 noon)

Noontime watch

Prayers during this hour are powerful if you need God to deliver you from difficult situations or from anyone that is oppressing you.

For example, If there are people in authority using their position to deal with you unfairly, this is the time to bring that person and situation before the Lord in prayer.

"Let everyone be subject to the governing authorities, for there is no authority except that which God has established. The authorities that exist have been established by God." (Romans 13:1)

Since authority is appointed by God, we must allow

Him to handle them if they are dealing with us righteously.

"The king's heart is in the hand of the LORD, as the rivers of water: he turneth it whithersoever he will." (Proverbs 21:1)

The 7th Watch (12 noon – 3pm)

Afternoon Prayers

During the time of this watch, Jesus was on the cross. It was at the climax of His ministry when He asked the Father to forgive others.

"The Jesus said, "Father, forgive them for they do not know what they do." (Luke 23:34)

We must use this hour to declare forgiveness to any and everyone who have done us wrong. While declaring forgiveness be sure not to be vague or general but be specific.

Remember forgiveness is for you, not for the person or persons that hurt or offended you.

In the Lord's Prayer when Jesus taught His disciples to prayer. He mentioned forgiveness as a key to effective prayer.

"And forgive us our debts as we have forgiven our debtors." (Matthew 6:12)

The 8th Watch (3pm – 6pm)

Midafternoon

This watch is the time to pray for anything that has been delayed or detained. This is the time of recovery and restoration of lost time.

When we have deemed things dead or finished God can make it alive

But Jesus beheld them and said unto them, with men this is impossible but with God all things are possible.

Read Matthew 20:1-9

In Matthew 20:1-9, The landowner did not mind whether you came in the morning or last in the evening. However, what mattered was that everyone got paid.

Pay time was during the eight watch. The last was paid first and the first was paid last. During this hour is the time when God turns things around.

PRAYER ESSENTIALS

So far, we have determined that there is a proper pattern of prayer. Now we must understand and discover some keys that are essential in prayer.

We can know how to pray. Your heart can be in the right position. You can know the names and character of God and apply them correctly.

Also, you can pray the right prayers at the right time. However, without these essentials you will not breakthrough.

In Matthew 16:19 it says: "I will give you the keys to the kingdom of heaven; whatever you bind on earth will be bound in heaven and whatever you loose on earth will be loosed in heaven."

In this verse, Jesus is telling His disciples that He is

giving them two essential keys and that is access and authority.

Access to the heavenly realm and authority to move, operate or shift in that realm.

Many people are defeated simply because they do not know their authority, or how to move or operate in that authority.

Therefore, when we pray, we do not pray with authority. Why? Because we do not know our right, so we end up praying defeated prayer.

The Lord says in Hosea 4:6, "My people are destroyed for the lack of knowledge."

During Jesus' ministry, He spent time teaching and training those that followed Him. I believe that during this time of training and teaching the disciples learned their identity in Christ.

Thus, they understood their authority and now was able to move and operate in the power God intended us to walk in.

Our greatest issue as believers facing crisis in our lives, is not that we lack power, but we lack knowledge of the power that we have.

In Luke 10:1, "Jesus appointed seventy and sent them two by two ahead of Him into every city and place where He himself was about to come."

Now in Luke 10:17, the seventy returned with joy saying, "Lord, even the demons are subject to us through Your name.

Now understand this, demons respond to authority. When you engage the enemy through warfare prayers, you must know your authority in Christ.

If you do not know your authority you will not get favorable results that will bring you joy like the disciples did.

Another prayer essential that you must have is faith. Faith means your conviction of the truth of anything.

Faith is also defined as confidence or trust in a person or thing. Faith is belief that is not based on proof.

The book of Hebrews chapter 11:1 tells us that, "Now faith is the substance of things hoped for the evidence of things not seen."

This faith that is essential for answered prayer is the faith that Elijah had when he shut up the heavens so there would be no rain.

The confidence that he spoke with believing that his words would be honored just because he said it.

"Therefore, I tell you, whatever you ask in prayer believe that you have receive it and it will be yours."

(Mark 11:24)

In this passage, believe means to think to be true, to be persuaded of, to credit, place confidence in.

So in other words, Mark 11:24 is saying therefore I tell you, whatever you ask in prayer think it to be true, or be fully persuaded that you have received it and it will be yours.

This is why Hebrews 11 says, "NOW Faith."

Now as in at the present time or moment without further delay, immediately.

PRAYER GUIDENCE

Enter into His gates with thanksgiving

- Heavenly Father, God of Abraham Jacob and Isaac.
- Thank you for sacrificing your only son for us.
- Thank you for loving us so that you gave your only son that we may have life and life more abundantly.
- Thank you Father that you are mindful of us.
- Thank you Lord for your grace and your mercy.
- Thank you Lord for the gift of the Holy Spirit, you are a father that gives good gifts.
- Thank you Holy Spirit for being our helper, our guide, our protector and our teacher.
- Thank you Holy Spirit that you are the spirit of truth.

- Thank you Jesus for you are our high priest,
- Thank you Jesus, You intercede to the Father on our behalf.
- Thank you for bearing witness for our sin.
- Thank you for you were without sin, but for us you became sin.
- Thank you Jesus for you are great, Holy is your name, powerful is your name. Every knee shall bow, and every tongue shall confess that you are God.

Enter into his courts with praise Psalm 100:4

- You are the Alpha & Omega
- You are the beginning and the end.
- You are the first and the last, from age to age you remain the same.
- You are the same yesterday today and forever.
- You are an unchanging God, a God that change not.
- You are what is and was and is to come.
- You are the Almighty God,
- You are the ancient of day. Oh Lord Jesus, you are the Most High, the Author and finisher of our faith.

- You are the rock of our salvation, in you we put our trust, because you are the way, the truth and the life, the resurrection and Life.
- You are the holy Lamb of God, Immanuel Lord with us.
- You are the wonderful counselor; you are the prince of peace.
- You are the Lord strong and mighty,
- You are the Lord God mighty in battle.
- You are our refuge,
- You are our pavilion.
- Thou oh Lord are a shield, the glory and the lifter of our heads.
- You are our safety and our dwelling place,
- You are our hiding place, our secret place.
- You are our salvation and our deliverer.
- You are Jehovah Gibbor,
- You fight our battles for us
- You are the King of Kings and the Lord of Lords
- You are Lord of Host, God of the angelic armies and ruler of the armies of heaven
- You are a God that keeps a covenant to a thousand generations to them that Love you.

- You are a yoke destroyer and a burden remover.
- Your yoke is easy, and your burden is light
- You are the Christ, Messiah, anointed King
- Your throne, O Lord is like a fiery flame
- Your love, Lord, reaches to the heavens your faithfulness to the skies.
- Your righteousness is like the highest mountains,
- your justice like the great deep
- You, Lord, preserve both people and animals.
- Your throne, O God, [c] will last forever and ever a scepter of justice will be the scepter of your kingdom
- You love righteousness and hate wickedness.

Agree with our adversary quickly

Father God we come before you thanking, and praising YOU, knowing YOU are the Most High God, you have no rival. We come before Your throne through the power of the Blood of Jesus the Christ. Lord, we confess we are guilty. Father God forgive us of our sins, transgressions, and our iniquities. Lord God let the motive of our heart's be pure. Let our actions be righteous before YOU. Father God every iniquity of our forefathers we bring before you Lord, we repent. Cleanse us, and our bloodline Lord God, of All things that are ungodly. We are sorry for the hidden sin of Murder in our lineage. Because of this sin someone's destiny was stolen. Which gave the enemy a right to steal our destiny we humbly ask Your forgiveness.

Every time I presented offerings to You with the wrong motive I repent. Silence the voice of these offerings that speaks against me in the Heavenly Courts by the Blood of Jesus the Christ. Father God I divorce myself from every hidden or unhidden evil, demonic covenant made by me or my ancestors. I command their works to be void and null through the power of the blood of Jesus the Christ. Every evil altar that my name is attached to. I declare it destroyed by Holy Fire and every evil portal open over my life is destroyed by the blood of the Lamb and Holy Fire. Every sin hidden or unhidden every transgression every iniquity known or unknown I eradicate from my bloodline. I break the power of the sacrifice by the power of the blood of Jesus the Christ our Lord Yeshua. Lord God Almighty release the power of the blood of Jesus the Christ to testify on my behalf. Open the book of Destiny and take every legal right from the enemy.

That would cause me not to fulfill my God-given purpose. I declare that you Lord God is the Lord of us all.

I declare that anything that the enemy can use against me in the Heavenly courts, I command it to be void and null. We act now with what the book of Destiny says about our lives. Open every hidden thing concerning our destinies and let it be revealed unto us. Show us clearly your God-given plan concerning our lives. Give us power and might to destroy the works of darkness that hinders our divine purposes.

God of Host, captain of the army of angels I ask that you to send out the angelic army to assist me. I call for the angels of marvelous help to help me accomplish that which you set me to do. I call for the mighty angels of War to contend with them who contend with me. I call forth ministering angels to minister to me even in my sleep. I call forth The Breaker to annihilate the evil bondages on my live. I bind every force of the enemy, evil spirits, principalities, demons, princes of darkness, human agents every high thing that exalts itself against the Most High God, and release them from their assignments concerning me. I declare that every stronghold has been broken. We call forth the spoilers to spoil the enemy of his wealth. I call for the Angels of abundant Harvest to release the wealth of the enemy into my hands. I declare that every yoke has been destroyed.

Lord God I humbly ask that you release Your Righteous right hand concerning me and my family. Renew in us a right spirit. Transform our minds and let this mind that was in Christ Jesus be in us. Holy God I ask that you release upon us the spirit of the Lord Jesus the Christ, the spirit of wisdom, the spirit of knowledge, the spirit of understanding, the spirit of counsel, the spirit of power and might. Father God let our purpose be to please you in all things Let our motives be pure. Give us a desire for you above our daily bread. Let men call us blessed. Let our children be blessed. Bless us with all spiritual blessings. I decree and declare that me and my household shall serve the Lord. I decree that we have a prosperous future even as a soul prosper. We prosper in health and wealth. I release healing ministering angels to eradicate every residue of sickness and illnesses of any kind in our bodies. I decree and declare that our bodies our souls and our spirit, every part of us, is in divine order according to the will of the Father Yahweh.

In Jesus Christ name Amen.

PRAYER FOR YOUR MARRIAGE

Lord God almighty marvelous are your works oh God. You have led your people in the dessert, a cloud by day and a pillar of fire by night. Everything that is set in place is sent in place by the power of your word. In the beginning you said let there be light and there was light. By the power of your word you spoke the whole world into existence and everything you made was good.

Lord as I boldly approach your throne of Grace I ask that you forgive me of anything that I have done that would prevent you from hearing my petition on behalf of my marriage and family, and those whom you have assigned my voice to. Father, I stand in the gap for the liars, the fornicators, the adulterers, and the prostitutes, all who have given the enemy legal access on the earth and I ask for forgiveness. I stand in agreement with your son that bear witness for us and I ask that you vindicate me of all accusations that the accuser has brought before your heavenly courts concerning my marriage and family.

I ask that you contend with them that contend with me, fight against those that fight against me. Be my shield and buckler and fight this battle for me. For thou or Lord are a shield for me the glory and the lifter of our heads. Send your angels out ahead of me, make every crooked path straight and every rough path smooth. Send the angels of war out on my behalf to help me in this battle for my marriages and families. Send the ministering angels out to minister to my husband that have gone astray. Give me victory over my enemies give me their neck, cause every plot and plan set against my marriage and family to fail. Let the enemy fall into the very pit and trap that they have crafted.

Your word says whatever we bind on earth shall be bound in heaven, whatever we loose on earth shall be loosed in heaven.

By the power and authority given unto me by Jesus Christ of Nazareth, son of the living God

- I bind the spirit of divorce,

- I bind the spirit of greed
- I bind the spirit of never satisfied
- In the Name of Jesus Christ son of the Living God
- I bind the spirit of Lust and perversion
- I bind the Spirit of Adultery
- I bind the Spirit of confession
- I bind every spirit of rejection and pride in the Name of Jesus Christ
- I bind every spirit of anger and frustration
- I bind every spirit of uncontrolled passion
- I bind every spirit of pornography in the name of Jesus Christ son of the living God
- In the name of Jesus Christ of Nazareth son of the living God
- I lose the spirit of love and sound mind
- I lose the spirit of patience and longsuffering
- I lose the spirit of Unity and gentleness

By the power and authority given unto me by Jesus Christ of Nazareth son of the Living God. I take authority of the airways and the atmosphere concerning my marriage and family now. I decree and declare that my marriage is holy and ordained by God. I decree and declare that the glory shall be revealed in it and through it. I declare and decree in the name of Jesus that this marriage and family is a representation of Christ and the church. I decree and declare that my husband is head of my house as Christ is head of the church. I pray that as the head of my home my husband shall have wisdom and will fear the Lord. Lord give this man of God revelation of the plans you have for our family. I decree and declare that I love my husband and I submit to him. I decree and declare that I am a virtuous woman, and my husband and children shall call me blessed. Father let the spirit of the Lord take over this marriage and family.

Let the spirit of wisdom, Knowledge and understanding rest upon my marriage and family like never before. Heavenly Father, In the name of Jesus Christ open the eye of our understanding,

Open our eyes that we can see, release us from spiritual blindness.

In the name of Jesus the Christ.

Engaging the enemy

- Lord you said in your word, that if we ask anything in the name of your son Jesus Christ you will do it.
- In the name of Jesus Christ, I ask that you let us possess the gate of the enemy.
- In the name of Jesus Christ let our enemy fall by their own counsel and cast them out.
- The evil that the enemy have crafted against my marriage and family, let it fail.
- In the name of Jesus Christ let confusion hit the camp of my enemy. Rebuke the heathen and destroy the wicked. Let my enemies be turned back. Expose every demonic force operating in the life of my marriage and family.
- Make them where they are not able to perform their intended evil to divide my marriage and family.
- In the name of Jesus Christ make my enemies tongue fall upon themselves.
- Lord stretch out your arm and deliver my marriage and rid us of all bondage.

- Let every pharaoh that would pursue my family and marriage be drowned in the sea.
- Let every spirit hiding from us be exposed in the name of Jesus Christ
- Every giant of the valley be destroyed in Jesus Christ
- I break the chariots of the enemies of the valley in the name of Jesus Christ.
- I release the sword of the Lord against the powers of hell in the name of Jesus Christ
- Every Goliath coming against my family and marriage, like David I take you down in the name of Jesus
- I command healing to our broken hearts
- I command healing to our intimacy
- I command healing to our friendship
- I command healing to our Love
- I command healing to our bodies in the Name of Jesus Christ.
- I command every good seed that has been planted concerning this marriage and family to bring forth fruit in the name of Jesus.
- I command every evil seed that was planted to be uprooted and destroyed.

- I command total restoration upon this marriage and Family in the name of Jesus.

PRAYER FOR WISDOM

Heavenly Father, God of Abraham Jacob and Isaac. Thank you for sacrificing your only son for us. Thank you for loving us so that you gave your only son that we may have life and life more abundantly. Thank you Father that you are mindful of us. Thank you Lord for your grace and your mercy. Thank you Lord for the gift of the Holy Spirit, you are a father that gives good gifts.

You are the Alpha & Omega. You are the beginning and the end. You are the first and the last, from age to age you remain the same. You are the same yesterday today and forever. You are an unchanging God, a God that change not.

Lord I come before you and ask that you forgive me for my sins and unrighteousness. I come up under the blood of Jesus that cleanses us from our sin. Whatever I have done that is not pleasing unto you in word thought or deed.

Lord you said in your word in Psalm 111:10 that the fear of the Lord is the beginning of wisdom, and all who live it have insight. Holy Spirit help us teach us to fear that we may get wisdom that we can live it and have insight.

Lord your word declares in proverbs 4:7 is the principal thing; that I must get wisdom and in all thy getting get understanding. Lord I am seeking to get wisdom and to understanding. Lord I will not be wise in my own eyes, I will fear you and depart form evil. I thank you Lord that it will be health to my body and strength to my bones.

I commit my works to you Lord establish my thoughts according to your will.

Lord your word says in Mark 11:24 if we ask it will be given, seek and we will find, knock and it will be open. Lord I humbly ask that you give me wisdom and understanding.

Understanding is a wellspring of life to him who has

it, but instructions of fools is folly. The hear of the wise teaches his mouth and adds learning to his lips. Lord as I submit my heart to you, I totally surrender my will to your ways. God, I need wisdom. I trust you Lord with all my heart, and I lean not unto my own understanding. In all my ways I acknowledge you Lord so that you may direct my pathway.

Father God in the name of your son Jesus Christ we ask that you bless me with wisdom. Lord as I fight for my marriage and Family, I need wisdom. So that I do not make foolish decisions. I need wisdom to help me navigate through all the information, opinions and suggestions concerning my marriage and family. Lord give me wisdom that my emotions will not override your will. Lord give me wisdom so that my folly will not lead me to regret.

Lord you said in your word that you have given us the keys to the kingdom and whatever we bind on earth will be bound in heaven, and whatever we loose on earth will be loose in heaven. In the name of Jesus, we bind the spirit of ignorance and the lack of knowledge. I bind confusion and double mindedness from over my life in the name of Jesus the Christ. Lord give me wisdom to discern hidden motives and demonic agendas that has been sent to sabotage victory in my marriage and family.

Lord give my wisdom to identify distractions and idle works. Lord give me wisdom to help me avoid weariness so that I will not grow weary in doing good. Lord give me wisdom go get over every obstacle that is sent my way seen or unseen. Lord give me wisdom that I will not fall victim to spiritual blindness. Open my yes Lord that I may see, remove the spiritual scales and cataracts from my eyes. Give me wisdom Lord to discern the plans and purposes that you have for me and my marriage and family.

I make a conscience decision today to blaze a new path for my life. Lord I ask that you give me wisdom because wisdom is key.

Lord I thank your for hearing my prayer, in the name of Jesus the Christ.

Amen.

PRAYER FOR VINDICATION AND ANGELIC HELP

Heavenly Father, God of Abraham Jacob and Isaac. Thank you for sacrificing your only son for us. Thank you for loving us so that you gave your only son that we may have life and life more abundantly. Thank you Father that you are mindful of us. Thank you Lord for your grace and your mercy. Thank you Lord for the gift of the Holy Spirit, you are a father that gives good gifts.

You are the Alpha & Omega. You are the beginning and the end. You are the first and the last, from age to age you remain the same. You are the same yesterday today and forever. You are an unchanging God, a God that change not.

Heavenly Father God of Abraham, Isaac and Jacob.

Your word says in Psalm 24 that the earth belongs to you Lord and everything in it. The world and all who live in it. For you founded it upon the seas and established it upon the waters. Who may ascend the hill of the Lord? Who may stand in your holy place? He who had a clean hand and a pure heart, who does not lift up his soul to and idol.

Lord was me, cleanse me purify me so that my hand may be clean and my heart pure before you Lord. Forgive me if we have lifted my soul to an idol.

Lord you said in your word that we must boldly approach your throne of grace that we may obtain mercy. With boldness I approach your throne of grace and appeal to you today, God of Host captain for the angelic armies and ruler of the armies of heaven. According to psalm 91:11 you shall give your angels charge over us, to keep us in our ways.

I cry out to you today asking for divine help from the angels that you have given charge over us. Command them oh Lord of host to help us in this battle for my marriage and family. Dispatch the angels assigned to my life. For your word says in Psalm 34:7 the angel of the Lord encamped round about them that fear him and delivered them. Lord I fear you.

Some trust in chariots and some in horses but I trust in the name of the Lord our God. Send your angels with a great sound of a trumpet and they shall gather together your elect from the four winds, from one end of heaven to the other.

Lord Jesus the Christ son of the living God you said in John 14:14 that I may ask anything in your name you will do it. In the name of Jesus the Christ. Lord have mercy on me on me. My home is under a great attack of the enemy who is trying to destroy the very institution of marriages that was set up by the Father.

I stand before your courts today to answer all accusations that the accuser has brought up against me. I am guilty as charged, but Lord I come up under the blood of Jesus that testifies on our behalf. Jesus the Christ son of the living God, bear witness for me today. Lord vindicate me today, rule on my behalf so that I may be able to go forward and do your will. Render judgement on our behalf so that we can fulfil what you have written of us in the book of books.

Render judgement on my behalf so that our marriage and family can be a testimony of your resurrection power. Restore my marriage and family Lord for you name sake so that your Son may be glorified. So that the people from all nations will know that you are a God that restores.

Lord I thank you for hearing my prayer and vindicating me. Thank you for dispatching divine help for me and my family.

In Jesus Name Amen

PRAYERS THAT ROUT DEMONS

Heavenly Father, Lord my Creator Holy is your name. Lord you are worthy of all the glory and praise. You are a good God; I call you Abba Father. Lord you are the Alpha and Omega, the beginning and the end. You are a righteous Judge, the Captain of the Army of Angels. You are the Lord strong and mighty; you are mighty in battle. Who can stand against you Lord?

Every knee shall bow, and every tongue shall confess that you are God. You reign on the just and the unjust. You are God of the living and not the dead. You sit high and look down low. The earth belongs to you oh Lord.

Lord you have no need of a bull from our stall or goat from our pens, for every animal of the forest belong to you, and the cattle on a thousand hills (Psalm 50:9-10) You oh Lord are the God that made the whole world and everything in it. You are the Lord of heaven and earth you do not live in temples built by human hands. You are not served by human hands as if you needed anything. Rather, it is you oh Lord that gives everyone life and breath and everything else. (Acts 17:24-25)

Lord I give you thanks and praise, marvelous are the works of your hands.

Thank you for your son Jesus the Christ. Thank you, Jesus, for the ultimate sacrifice that you have made. You were without sin but for us you became sin. Lord we thank you that you are faithful. Lord you are righteous, and you are just.

Thank you that you are Jehovah Jireh the Lord that provide. Thank you that you are Jehovah Rapha our healer. Thank you that you are Jehovah Nissi our banner. Thank you that you are Jehovah Gibbor The might God.

Lord we thank you for the covenant of marriage that you have created and made with us. Thank you Lord that you are a covenant keeper, you keep covenant to one thousand generations to them that Love you.

Lord God Almighty I humbly come before your

throne of grace that we my obtain mercy. Lord, I repent before you of my sin, transgression and my iniquity. Wash me from the crown of my head to the soul of my feet. Lord I present my body to you a living sacrifice may I be holy and acceptable to you which is my reasonable service.

Lord whatever unforgiveness I am harboring in my heart against anyone that has hurt, reject or offend my, I forgive them now and release them from my heart. Lord I cover myself with the blood of Jesus Christ, I cover my home and family, my possessions and everything that is connected to me.

Lord let the fire of God surround and protect our lives from destruction. Lord hide us under the shadow or your wing. Hide the location of my attack making it difficult for me to be picked up in the realm of the spirit from demonic forces of evil.

Let the angel of the Lord encamp around me and my family and dispatch the warring angels to assist me in battle. For the name of the Lord is a mighty strong tower. The righteous run into it and are safe. Lord let me dwell in the land of safely.

Lord lead me safely and I will not fear. Let the sea overwhelm my enemies.

In the shadow of your wing I will trust.

Cover my head in the day of battle.

Cover me with your feathers.

Be my defense and our refuge.

Heavenly Father Lord of Abraham Isaac and Jacob. Let your power be released from your hand.

Let the Power of your anger be released against the power of darkness

Lord you have given us power and authority over the power of the enemy.

I will trample upon snakes and scorpions and nothing shall harm me.

I will stand on behalf of my marriage and family and take authority over every evil work operating against us and I cancel it now in the name of Jesus.

Every plant that the Father above have not planted my marriage and family I rooted it up now.

I lay the ax to the root of every evil tree in my marriage and family.

Spear of the Lord, locate and destroy every enemy of my marriage and family and destroy it in the name of Jesus.

Spear of the Lord, arise and send confusion into the camps of the enemy in the name of Jesus.

Lord let the confidence of the enemy operating against my marriage and family be rooted out in Jesus name.

Let all spirits rooted in rejection be plucked up now in Jesus name.

Let all spirits rooted in hurt and trauma be rooted up now in Jesus name.

Every demonic seed planted to bring blindness to my husband be uprooted now in Jesus name.

Let all spirits rooted in fear be uprooted now in Jesus name.

Every demonic cycle operating in my marriage and family be disrupted and stopped now.

Lord I call down holy fire from heaven to consume demonic altars that have been set up against my marriage and family.

Lord your word says that we shall decree a thing and it shall be established for us. In the name of Jesus the Christ I decree that my marriage is healed and made whole.

I decree that I have a mind of Christ, my husband have a mind of Christ my children have a mind of Christ. We are blessed and we have favor with God and man.

In Jesus Name.

Amen.

ABOUT THE AUTHOR

A Servant of the Most High God, Meltoria Woodside, is happily married to Yocasta Woodside, and is a mother to three wonderful sons. She was born in The Bahamas.

This seasoned entrepreneur offers online coaching services for married women to get them through the "tough patches of marriages" that she herself has overcome.

"Over 10 years ago, I was faced with infidelity in my marriage. It was one of the toughest seasons of my entire life. Although I had reason and right to leave, I decided to stay and push through.

Along with infidelity, I endured verbal, emotional and physical abuse.

"However, with the help of the Lord, I was able to fight through all of that, and conquer what many would consider a lost cause.

Now, my husband is saved and delivered, and my family is now experiencing what I believe are some of the best days ever.

"For my accomplishments with my marriage with the help of Holy Spirit, I am qualified to do what I am doing with ministry," she testifies.

Meltoria obtained her associate degree in Ministry, bachelor's degree in theology and is a certified marriage coach.

Because of her passion for discipleship, Meltoria has helped married women to not only position themselves mentally and emotionally to get through the most trying times of their lives, but to also recognize their purpose.

"Through my ministry, many women have matured spiritually, growing closer in their relationship with the Lord, and also homes have been saved from divorce," she attests.

Moreover, as she has been appointed by God to nations, Meltoria has been commissioned to uproot and tear down, to destroy and overthrow, and to build and to plant according to Jeremiah 1:10.

Over the course of her life, Meltoria has been involved in ministry for more than 15 years. She has served as a youth pastor, a dance minister, and now she operates in the fivefold ministry as a Prophet.

Meltoria is also the author of "When Wives Fight Families Win" and "Fight to Win: A Battle Plan to Fight for Your Marriage."

This aggressive, bold and compassionate woman is willing to go against popular opinion and stand on what she believes, speaking boldly and truthfully about what God has authorized her to speak about.

Based on her own experience, she recognizes that the topic of marriage is a sensitive one, amidst telling people to stay and fight through the hell they may be experiencing.

Nevertheless, Meltoria has overcome those trying times in her marriage, and is a testimony today of what God can do and how He can do the same for you.

Future goals for this mighty woman of God are to complete her Ph.D. in Ministry with a focus on family counseling and publish more books,

OTHER BOOKS BY THE AUTHOR.

❖

When Wives Fight Families Win

❖

Fight to Win

"A battle plan to fight for your marriage and family"

❖

Healing & Deliverance

For the Broken Wife.

Made in the USA
Las Vegas, NV
15 March 2025